PERFECTING YOU!

THE FACETS OF SINGLENESS
CHRISTIAN JOURNAL

DR. ISAIAH EUGENE KEYS

Perfecting YOU!
The Facets of Singleness
Christian Journal

Copyright 2025 Isaiah Eugene Keys

All rights reserved. No part of this publication may be reproduced, distributed or transmitted in any form or by any means, without prior written permission. Unless otherwise identified, scripture quotations are from the King James Version of the Bible.

Published by
Dreamer Reign, LLC
P.O. Box 291354
Port Orange, FL 32129

www.dreamerreign.com

For Worldwide Distribution
Printed in the U.S.A.

ISBN: 978-1-952253-50-8

CONTENTS

Introduction 4
Chapter 1: Are you Single? 7
Chapter 2: Singleness is the First Step 13
Chapter 3: Don't Overlook Your Single Season 21
Chapter 4: God and You 29
Chapter 5: Who Am I?: Discovering You 37
Chapter 6: Seasons of Singleness 45
Chapter 7: Pressures of being Single 51
Chapter 8: Confronting You 61
Chapter 9: Alone vs. Lonely 69
Chapter 10: Dating 77
Chapter 11: Prayer and Accountability 85
Chapter 12: Current Trends In Dating 91
Chapter 13: Encouraging Messages for Singles 99
Chapter 14: Dating and Marriage Goals 107
Scriptures 114
References 125

INTRODUCTION

Singleness, what is it all about? All around the world right now someone is single, has been single, or is about to be single. We all entered this world single. I don't believe anyone came out of the womb dating someone or married, but anything is possible. Nevertheless, there could be many reasons why someone is single: maybe you lost a spouse, are divorced, just got out of a relationship, never been in a relationship, or you're planning to never get married. Whatever category of single you fall under, there is purpose in your singleness and this journal is for you.

This journal was written to encourage you and provide you with tools for a successful single season. Much of what I write about in this journal I have discovered, experienced, and been taught in my single seasons. With that being said, I am not just a writer, but also a partaker of encouragement and tools with you. Even as I wrote, it provoked self-examination and accountability. Revealing places where I can improve. Growing up in church (Church Boy lol), my view and understanding of singleness was unclear. Marriage was always promoted and championed, but what happens before that? What should be happening before marriage was never clearly defined. It wasn't until I was in my mid-thirties that I began to realize that there is purpose in singleness. I had dated before and had several single seasons, but this particular season was different. God brought me to a place of isolation for the purpose of discovering me.

Sometimes we can get so busy with life we can lose who we are, or not even know who we are. Someone once asked me, "Are you ready to get married?" I quickly answered, "Yes!" I answered out of fear of what they would say if I said no; I felt obligated to answer yes because there would be something wrong with me if I wasn't ready to get married. Right? Later, my answer bothered me and continued to throughout the day. Now, I could have just ignored it, but I chose to confront myself with truth. The truth was, at that time, I did not want to get married and was not ready. I wasn't ready to let go of my single season. I couldn't let go because the purpose for this season was not yet fulfilled. I started to realize who I was as an individual still needed some work. I also enjoyed being single, and there is nothing wrong with that. God was and is perfecting me.

The purpose of God's perfecting is not to make us unflawed, but bring us to a whole person. A whole person is one that is unbroken mentally, emotionally, and spiritually. Through God's perfecting process, He matures us emotionally, mentally, and spiritually, bringing us to the mature place of wholeness. As I now reflect on my singleness journey, it's been a challenging and enlightening journey for me, that is still currently happening. Love for God, myself, my future wife, family, and others keeps me moving forward and submitted to God's perfecting process. From dealing with past trauma to the breaking of generational curses, God has been unraveling the grave clothes that have held me bound. Join me on this journey in and through singleness. I pray this journal opens your eyes to the riches found in singleness and relationships. Now, there is much to uncover and much to do; let's get to work!

Throughout this journal I will mention the word "dating." There are various ideas and perspectives about dating. Therefore, to eliminate any confusion, dating in this journal is defined as a relationship where two people spend regular time together with the intention of getting to know each other. Dating in the kingdom of God is not a sexual relationship, but rather a time to gather information in order to evaluate compatibility, and possibly to commit to a more serious relationship.

I believe before any dating begins, a friendship should be formed. The decision to promote that friendship to dating or anything further should be given to God. A more serious type of dating, I define as courting. Courting is dating with the intention of marriage. Overall, every connection you make, whether friends, or dating, you are connecting with a brother or sister in Christ. Maintaining this mindset will help you be successful in your dating process.

Chapter One

Are you **Single?**

"A double minded man is unstable in all his ways" James 1:8

Many people entering into dating relationships claim to be single. A status of "single" is a prerequisite for a dating relationship most would agree—but many are not truly single. You might be asking yourself, "How does someone make the mistake of labeling themselves single?" Consider this: *"Single is not simply defined as an absence of physical connection to someone, but the status of single defines your emotional, spiritual, and physical state as well…are you single emotionally, spiritually, and physically? Many people are in relationships or even married to fear, bitterness, rejection, hurt, pride, their way, their past, and various things that hinder relationships and marriages from working. Being married to these things will produce dysfunctional and toxic behavior that will break*

Perfecting YOU!

any relationship you desire to have."

— **Dr. Roy Etienne Smith**
President, Isaiah University Holy Spirit Seminary

Therefore, it's imperative in your single season to examine your relationship status. Are you truly single? Unwillingness to let go of the aforementioned significant others is evidence of a relationship. For example, someone in a marriage with fear listens to it, consults it before making decisions, is influenced by it, and trusts it. They have made an agreement unknowingly with fear to love, cherish, and obey it until death does them part. Your single season is a perfect time to get a divorce! Break free from these agents of disorder, and be married to love, joy, peace, grace, faith, and much more in God. Fruitful relationships and marriages start with God.

JOURNAL SECTION

Perfecting YOU!

Are you single?

Perfecting YOU!

Chapter Two

Singleness is the *first step*

The word single can be defined as "individual," complete, or whole. Singleness should be pursued and not avoided. In the number system, you can't get to any other number before going to and through one. The number one is the foundation for getting to the numbers that follow. You can't get two, three, four, or any other number until you get one. Usually, the first step in any process puts you in position to complete the following steps. If the first step puts you in position, then without it, the following steps cannot truly be completed because you're not in the proper position to complete them. When building a house, the first step is to build the foundation. The strength of the foundation is indicative of the house's strength. A faulty foundation will neither stand nor have longevity.

Perfecting YOU!

The Bible gives us a perfect illustration of this in the book of Matthew 7:24-27(NIV): *"Therefore everyone who hears these words of mine and puts them into practice is like a wise man who built his house on the rock. 25 The rain came down, the streams rose, and the winds blew and beat against that house; yet it did not fall, because it had its foundation on the rock. 26 But everyone who hears these words of mine and does not put them into practice is like a foolish man who built his house on sand. 27 The rain came down, the streams rose, and the winds blew and beat against that house, and it fell with a great crash."*

Your single season is the foundation for your future marriage. When you enter into a marriage, you are an individual. If you as an individual are broken, you will be constructing that relationship on a foundation that's similar to sand. That marriage will have difficulty standing. Now, your foundation can be fixed while in a marriage, but it will be challenging. Who you are as a single person will be revealed in the marriage. Therefore, you should ask yourself a series of important questions, "Do I like myself?" "Would I want to be Married to me?" "Do I like being around myself?" "Do I love me?" If your answer to those questions is no, it's okay, you just have some work to do. If you're coming back into a single season from a relationship or marriage it's an opportunity for evaluating your foundation. These are some questions you may ask: What condition is my foundation in? Are there cracks in my foundation caused by the relationship I was in? Or was that there prior to the relationship? How can I strengthen my foundation? By the end of this journal my prayer is that you're able to position yourself on the path towards the change you seek. You can do it!

"Your Marriage will only be as good as your singleness." — **Dr. Myles Munroe**

JOURNAL SECTION

Singleness is the First Step

Perfecting YOU!

Singleness is the First Step

Perfecting YOU!

Chapter Three

Don't overlook your *single season*

What does it mean to be single? When you hear the word single what first comes to mind? The word single can refer to the quantity of something, a status, or a play in baseball. In the world of dating and relationships the word single is used to describe someone's relationship status. In the contemporary world, social status holds significant importance. Status is your rank or position, which could be social, professional, or any other area a ranking can be determined. Whether it's a Facebook status, financial status, or the status of your reputation people tend to judge you based on your status.

Perfecting YOU!

Oftentimes the single status is despised, prompting single people to also despise it. Single people will spend their entire single season looking for that "special someone." Generally speaking, relationships are celebrated, as they should be. However, they should not be celebrated for the purpose of diminishing singleness or making it insignificant. Your single season has purpose. God gave us the seasons of Fall, Winter, Summer, and Spring. Each season has a purpose and is needed. In each season, so many things take place that we need and creation needs in order to grow. In the Fall, the leaves fall off the trees, which is preparation for new growth in the Springtime. If we just skip over Fall, we will never experience new growth. In the same way there is purpose in the single season.

There are things that need to happen in your single season that promotes growth and prepares you for the next season. Most single people are missing out on the treasures of wisdom, understanding, knowledge, and maturity that are found in the season of singleness, due to their focus being solely on the next thing. Their minds are occupied with wondering questions such as: When will I find the one? How can I be in a relationship? When will it be my time to get married? Celebrate your singleness. Being single is a time to become an individual. Each of us has been uniquely designed by God. Your time of being single is the time to discover that uniqueness, accept it, learn how to walk in it, and be confident in who you are. Like your body, every part is distinct, but working and functioning in the body to keep it operating effectively. Therefore, when you are working and functioning properly as an individual, your relationships — including marriage — are more likely to be productive and healthy.

JOURNAL SECTION

Don't Overlook Your Single Season

Perfecting YOU!

Don't Overlook Your Single Season

Perfecting YOU!

Chapter Four

God and *you*

Your single season is a time to build and strengthen your relationship with God. It's a time to find and strengthen your purpose and identity in Him. Without identity and purpose, a fulfilling life is unreachable. Therefore, it's imperative that in your single season you strengthen your relationship with God. God is the foundation of your true purpose and identity. Only through relationship can we understand our Creator's purpose for ourselves. The book of Genesis contains records of beginnings. Man (Adam) and woman (Eve) were form ed and made. Before Adam and Eve were brought together, they spent time with God and had a relationship with Him. Therefore, Adam and Eve both spent time with God before meeting each other. This time spent with God was intimate time. The more intimacy a relationship has, the stronger it will be. Intimacy is defined as closeness or familiarity. God was intimate with every detail of Adam and Eve. Adam and Eve reciprocated this and were intimate with God. The word "Eden" in the Garden of Eden, means "delightful place." Adam and Eve were constantly in the presence of God and were naked. This is showing us God's original intent for a relationship with Him. We were not created to hide or be estranged from God, but just the opposite. God requires transparency from us; He desires us to be close and very familiar with Him. Intimate with the details of Him as He is with us.

In Genesis 17, we see this requirement from God spoken to Abraham. God appears to Abraham and said, "I am God Almighty; walk before Me faithfully and be blameless. Then I will make My covenant between Me and you and will greatly increase your numbers." God taught Abraham how to walk before Him. The word walk in this passage is referring to Abraham's life. His ways, comings and goings, etc. In other words, God was saying, do not hide anything from Me, be transparent with Me, and be faithful in doing this. Walking faithfully and blamelessly before God results in a covenant relationship with Him. Before any marital covenant is entered into, there should be a covenant with God. Covenant with God is and should be the foundation of any marital covenant. Covenant with God brings fruitfulness and multiplication in every area of our lives. It brings forth the fruit of the spirit: love, joy, peace, longsuffering gentleness, goodness, faith, meekness, and temperance. It matures and shapes your character, making you more like Him.

Therefore, in your single season, it's crucial that you spend quality time with God. God requires us to walk unhidden and openly before Him, which will produce constant growth and fruit in our lives. Like Abraham, through covenant with God you will be blessed in order to be a blessing. We are always growing in relationship with God. Whether your relationship is in the beginning stages or you have been in a relationship with God for years, your single season is a great opportunity to strengthen your relationship with Him.

JOURNAL SECTION
Time with God

God and You

Perfecting YOU!

God and You

Perfecting YOU!

Chapter Five

Who am I?:
Discovering you

"And the vessel that he made of clay was marred in the hand of the potter: so he made it again another vessel, as seemed good to the potter to make it."
Jeremiah 18:4

You were fearfully and wonderfully made, uniquely designed by God. Your intricate makeup reveals the complexity in which He made you. Most people go through life with a basic knowledge of themselves, and never progress in that knowledge. Some never even obtain a basic knowledge of themselves. Then there are some that have a good understanding and knowledge of who they are. Self-discovery is an ongoing process. Therefore, whether you are just beginning to know who you are or revisiting yourself, self-discovery is an essential ingredient for growth. To know yourself produces confidence and security in who you are. It also produces love

Perfecting YOU!

for yourself and your Creator. Your personality, idiosyncrasies, height, weight, race, the good, bad, and ugly about yourself, is what makes you unique and extraordinary. Knowing who you are eliminates the fear of people's opinions or criticism. It eliminates insecurities that tell you to conform to whatever people are pleased with, which hold you back from being yourself. Knowing who you are stimulates growth and maturity. You are worth the time it takes to get to know yourself. God knows every detail about you, even things you have yet to discover about yourself. Therefore, if God loves you this much, you should love what He loves. Knowing, embracing, and accepting who you are is loving yourself. Your favorite color, food, season, month of the year, or hobby may seem insignificant, but they are important elements that make up you.

In the book of Jeremiah, God sent the prophet Jeremiah down to the potter's house. There Jeremiah noticed clay on the potter's wheel, which was marred in the potter's hands. Marred meaning impaired or disfigured. God wanted Jeremiah to tell the nation of Israel that they were like this clay in His hands. God wanted Israel to see and know that He was in control of their lives and has the power and authority to do what seems best for them. *"And the vessel that he made of clay was marred in the hand of the potter: so he made it again another vessel, as seemed good to the potter to make it." Jeremiah 18:4*

As you get to know yourself, you must embrace and accept who you are in totality. You must come to and accept the reality that you're going to have issues, and that's okay. God is your Potter. He will continue to mold you and make you as you offer up your life to Him. Begin your journey to discovering yourself. You will discover things along the way that are awesome, and some things that will make you cringe. It's for you to just accept and love who you find, as God does. God loves you with the knowledge of every mistake you would make, every issue you would have, and every problem you would struggle with. When this unconditional love is accepted from God, it gives you the capacity to love yourself in the same way that He does. Love yourself with the love of God. Embrace, accept, and love who you are, because God does.

"God loves us the way we are, but too much to leave us that way."

Perfecting YOU!

Below are some activities and questions to help you get to know yourself better. Consider these activities and questions as you journal. If you have answered these questions before, revisit them. They might have changed. You are not limited to the questions below. You can always add more lists or questions. These questions are just to get you started. Enjoy your discovery!

Make a list of your:
1. Pet peeves
2. Passions
3. Hobbies
4. Favorite color(s)
5. Favorite movie(s)
6. Favorite tv show(s)
7. Favorite song(s)
8. Favorite season(s)

Questions to ask yourself:
1. What angers you? And why?
2. Who do you admire? And why?
3. What standards do you live by?
4. What do you value? And why?
5. What are your strengths?
6. What are your weaknesses?

JOURNAL SECTION
Get to know you.

Perfecting YOU!

Who am I?: Discovering You

Perfecting YOU!

Chapter Six

Seasons of *singleness*

There are seasons of singleness, like Fall, Winter, Spring, and Summer. Every season is different, but each season is preparation for the next one. There can be seasons of isolation. Isolation is not a season where you have no friends or people around you, but it's a season where God has strategically placed certain people in your life for the purpose of growth. These people are there to sharpen you and vice versa. This is not typically a season of dating, but working on your relationship with God, you, and learning how to have proper relationships with people. Another season would be a season of dating. This could be courting (dating for marriage) connecting for the purpose of establishing friendships, or dating just to see what is out there. It's a time to discover and solidify

Perfecting YOU!

what you want in a relationship.

What type of person do you like? What attributes or characteristics do you like in people? Dating will also reveal your character. Dating can be very informative and a stimulus for growth if done with the right motivations, maturely, and with accountability. Another season of singleness is preparation for marriage. Overall, every season is preparing for marriage if that is your desire. Although, not everyone desires to be married. This is spoken about in 1 Corinthians 7. Paul explained that marriage and singleness is a gift from God. The apostle Paul desired those that were widowed or unmarried to remain like him, if they couldn't he requested that they marry. He explained that everyone has their gift from God, and everyone can't be like him.

Therefore, some will not get married and this is fine as long as God has given you the grace to do so. Giving you grace means God has equipped you with the ability to live a single life. On the other hand, if your desire is to get married there is a season of preparation for that. In this season you are dating and courting with the intent of getting married. There are various reasons why someone is single. Some are single because of divorce or loss of a spouse. Some are single and plan to never get married again. Whatever season you are in prayerfully seek God for direction and clarity on what season you are in. Even if your desire is never to get married, God still has purpose for you in your singleness.

JOURNAL SECTION

Reflect on what season of singleness you are or were in.

Perfecting YOU!

Seasons of Singleness

Perfecting YOU!

Chapter Seven

The pressures of *being single*

In society, single people are inundated with pressures to find that "special someone" in order to start the journey to marriage. Singles give many the opportunity to live out their dreams of being a matchmaker, which in some cases can work out for your good! Singles can deal with pressures of sexual frustration, lust, fear, rejection, and insecurities just to name a few. Being single sometimes carries a negative connotation, depending on various circumstances. If you're in your 30s and older the pressure really heats up. At every family gathering, hanging out with friends, you get asked these questions "Why are you still single?" "When are you getting married?" "When are you going to start dating"? or "When are you getting married again"? As if you can just wave your hand and make your single status change. Many succumb to the pressures and become anxious about their future, constantly asking these questions "Will I ever get married?" Will I ever find someone?" "Is there something wrong with me?" By allowing these pressures from peers and society to weigh on your mind and thoughts you may force yourself into relationships or even a marriage prematurely. Any relationship entered into in that state, is built upon what people will say or do if you don't do this. The foundation is fear and anxiety. Fear of what people are going to think if you are still single in your 30s or 40s, anxious about the future asking what if? Unfortunately, many marriages have been built on a sand-like foundation. With this in mind, courting should be carefully entered into with much prayer. God gave us access to wisdom and discernment to properly guide us in this process.

The pressure of people should not sway you in any direction. If their opinions and questions are able to move you from a place of faith into places of fear, anxiety, insecurities, rejection, envy, jealousy, discontentment, inadequacy, or any other damaging or hindering place, you are not secure in your singleness. Singles also are often overlooked, which can invoke many of these feelings and emotions. Many events in churches are for married people. Sometimes directly or indirectly alienating singles. Singles can be an afterthought many times on holidays such as Valentine's Day, which highlight couples. This feeling of being alienated often invites rejection into your life and can cause you to devalue singleness. Know this, that being single is not a curse or a negative thing. Being single should be enjoyed and valued. Be secure in it and cherish it. Below I highlighted some emotions and feelings I have felt along with other singles:

Fear

1. Fear of never finding someone. Focus on finding you first, the rest will fall into place from this starting point.
2. Fear of people being disappointed in you if you don't get married. Marriage should not define your worth, know your worth as an individual.
3. Fear of trusting again or allowing someone into your life. Trust God in the process, He will direct your paths.
4. Fear of messing it all up or making a mistake. At the end of failure is success, don't be afraid to fail.
5. Fear of sinning against God. We walk by faith, not Fear.

Envy or Discontentment

1. Not being satisfied, happy, or content in your singleness. This can be a distraction, changing your focus from the purpose of singleness to constantly thinking about what is after singleness. Always asking what's next? This leads to jumping into relationships or marriage prematurely and with the wrong person. In the end these premature relationships will not satisfy or fix discontentment. You have to first be content with who you are and satisfied with yourself, that you are enough. You must be satisfied in God and in who He is.

Perfecting YOU!

   Trust that where He has you right now, is the right place for you.
2. Despising those who are in relationships. If you can't value other people's relationships. How will you ever value your own? Value and respect others and their relationships.

Insecurities about being single

1. Being influenced by opinions, comments, and unsound advice about your singleness. Being single is not a negative position, but a necessary position in order to move forward.
2. Always feeling the need to defend your singleness to family, friends, and those who are in relationships. Be comfortable and confident in your single season. Trust the process of God and where he has you in this season.
3. Accepting friendship from anyone having no standards for yourself and who you let into your life. Your life has value, who you connect with is important.
4. Changing in order for someone to like you. Who you are should be enough for you and others.

Pride

1. Not being teachable, ignoring advice from credible and spirit led believers. It's important to adhere to advice and counsel from those who have gone through the process and who God has placed in your life for leadership.
2. Believing that you don't have to do any work to be in a

relationship. To be in a relationship is a gift, as well as being single. Relationships are valuable and anything of value requires effort and work.

JOURNAL SECTION

The Pressures of Being Single

Perfecting YOU!

The Pressures of Being Single

Perfecting YOU!

Chapter Eight

Confronting *you*

It's time to step into the ring! It's time to confront you! As we go through life our experiences sometimes leave us injured emotionally and mentally. Sometimes we are unaware that we were injured and sometimes we are aware, but because of the pain we ignore our injuries or avoid dealing with them altogether. In addition, those injuries prevent success and productivity in our lives. The first and most difficult step toward healing and wholeness is confronting these injured places. If you have ever had a serious physical injury before, you know there is a time for resting. You also know that, there is a time to move and strengthen what was injured and recover its original functionality. In the above analogy, "injuries" could represent broken relationships that hurt you, or trauma from childhood experiences, etc… Similar to a physical injury, where you might go see a doctor, get x-rays, rest from activity for a while, and go to rehab, the same needs to happen if you are injured emotionally or mentally. We have the great Counselor, the Holy Spirit, who leads us into all truth and helps us heal. However, sometimes the Holy Spirit will work through counselors or therapists to get you to the place of healing. With that being said, allow the Holy Spirit to lead you in the right direction.

There is nothing wrong with therapy or counseling when it is needed. You want to be in the right position for relationships and marriage, healed and whole. Your single season is the time and opportunity to work these things out. Nonetheless, as previously mentioned the goal is not to reach an unflawed state, but wholeness. Wholeness is having dominion over what injured you. You rule it, instead of it ruling you. Yes, there may be scars and adjustments you had to make as a result of the injury, yet you conquered it. You took back your power and overcame it. When it no longer has power over you, that is wholeness. To begin the process of becoming whole, confrontation is necessary. Confrontation produces awareness of self. A lack of awareness can be detrimental to growth. For example, have you ever neglected to clean or maintain something in your house? Usually, things that go uncleaned become saturated with dust, dirt, and all kinds of things. Household appliances and machines that are not maintained either stop working, break, or are just no longer usable. That is what happens when we neglect areas of our lives that we know need attention. Additionally, there are areas in our lives that need attention that we are not even aware of. Confron-

Confronting You

tation brings awareness and attention to those neglected areas, which if left unattended, can cause havoc in our personal lives. No one wants to live or visit an unclean house. Confrontation will ensure you maintain a healthy life that attracts people and will not repel them. Confrontation has helped stimulate growth in my personal life. It is very easy to ignore and put things that necessitate our attention away out of sight. These places that need confrontation are key to our success and growth. This is why it is so difficult to do, not many of us are willing to submit to confrontation. When I started to confront things in my life, I started to see change happen, and it's an ongoing process. The treasures found in confrontation are invaluable. Step into the ring by faith, not fear, because you will win!

What are you confronting? An attitude, behavior, or a way of thinking? This month keep track of what you're confronting and your progress. Part of confronting is finding the root cause of the behavior, attitude, or way of thinking.

This can be painful and taxing, but through the guidance of the Holy Spirit, who leads us into all truth, we can reach the necessary places of healing and wholeness.

JOURNAL SECTION

What are you confronting?

Confronting You

Perfecting YOU!

Confronting You

Perfecting YOU!

Chapter Nine

Alone vs. Lonely

"...for he hath said, I will never leave thee, nor forsake thee."
Hebrews 13:5

Many times, the words "alone" and "lonely" are used interchangeably, or thought to have the same meaning. However, these two words are not identical, and understanding how they are different will aid in promoting healthy singleness. The word alone refers to a person's physical state. If someone says "I am alone right now", they are saying no one is around them. The word lonely refers to a person's emotional state. It is a feeling of disconnection or unhealthy isolation. You can feel lonely in the middle of a crowd of people and even with friends. The feeling of loneliness is sometimes evidence of emotional damage.

Perfecting YOU!

Therefore, it's okay to be alone at times, but it is not okay to be lonely. Oftentimes that damage was caused by dysfunctional relationships. Dysfunctional relationships, in simple terms, are relationships that are unhealthy. We know that if a person continues to eat unhealthy food, they are damaging their body and will eventually become sick. Dysfunctional relationships feed our emotional person unhealthy food and we will eventually get sick. Those types of relationships will produce rejection, insecurities, trust issues, and self-hate, which all can contribute to feeling lonely. As a believer we have access to an abundance of life in God. In the book of John chapter 10 verse 10, Jesus states *"…I am come that they might have life, and that they might have it more abundantly."* If you were damaged emotionally, you don't have to stay damaged.

Through Jesus Christ, you have access to an abundance of life. When you acknowledge the damage and submit it to God, it allows healing to begin in those damaged places. God needs to be the Healer of any damage in your life. Marriage will not heal loneliness. A relationship will not heal loneliness, but a healthy relationship with God will. As previously mentioned, use this time of singleness to strengthen your relationship with God because all other relationships should and will be built upon it. Healthy relationships in the Kingdom of God have God as their foundation. Trust God and allow Him access into the innermost places of your life, so that you can be whole and healthy in all areas of your life. Do the necessary work to be whole for those present and future relationships.

JOURNAL SECTION

Are you lonely?

Alone vs. Lonely

Perfecting YOU!

Alone vs. Lonely

Perfecting YOU!

Chapter Ten

Dating

Dating can be a confusing thing to figure out. Most of our understanding of dating has been influenced by friends, movies, tv shows, songs, observations, or experiences. Those influences mold and shape our ideas and thoughts about dating. We live in an age where we are inundated with information. At the tip of your fingers, you have access to an abundance of teachers and influencers with information on any topic you can think of. It can be difficult navigating through all of that. Trying to figure out who is right or what information you should follow can be exhausting and frustrating. That being said, it is imperative that you seek God for guidance and direction during this process.

Perfecting YOU!

He will help you navigate through the dating process; connecting you with the right people and information that will provide you with sound counsel and accountability. One key element to have during your dating process is purpose. Purpose is the reason something is done. When things are done without purpose it leaves the door open for anything to happen. Purpose brings order and establishes the necessary boundaries for success. It will also expose those relationships that will only hinder you because they don't align with your purpose. What is your reason? What is your desired result? What are your goals? What outcome are you looking for? These are some questions to ask yourself when starting to define your purpose for dating. Being aware of your reason for existence, why God created you, or what He created you to do on this earth should also be considered when establishing your purpose for dating.

Understanding your God-given purpose will directly affect who you connect with or date. Purpose gives you vision for your life. Some people will not line up with that vision. These could be great people; they are just not headed in the same direction as you. God, who is our example of doing things, does everything on purpose. He is never random and He always gets His desired result or outcome. For example, in the book of Genesis God's plan to bring forth the nation of Israel was revealed. God chooses Abraham and Sarah for the purpose of bringing forth the nation of Israel. Through the nation of Israel came Jesus Christ, who brought us salvation. Therefore, purposeful connections and relationships will not only benefit you, but also those around you. Now, there might be mistakes and missteps along the way, which is okay. Nevertheless, if a purpose is in place, it will minimize mishaps and guide you safely to your destination.

JOURNAL SECTION
What is your purpose?

Dating

Perfecting YOU!

Dating

Perfecting YOU!

Chapter Eleven
Prayer and *accountability*

"Trust in the LORD with all your heart and lean not on your own understanding; in all your ways submit to him, and he will make your paths straight"
Proverbs 3:5-6 (NIV)

Prayer is a vital part of the believer's life. A simple definition of prayer is "communication with God." Communication is a way of life; nothing would get accomplished without the ability to communicate with each other. Whether it be verbal or non-verbal we are all communicating with one another every day. We can and should do the same with God. Good communication builds and strengthens relationships. During your single season it's important to establish your prayer life and keep good communication with God. Make sure you are speaking with God and hearing what He is saying. A good

Perfecting YOU!

prayer life will help you navigate through this season of your life and future seasons. Good communication with God will bring clarity and direction in your single season. Prayer is like charging your phone. Without charging your phone, it will eventually die. Prayer keeps you charged and full of life. You will have the most productive and fruitful single season by maintaining a good prayer life.

Accountability is also a key part of this. Accountability is giving an account for your actions as it pertains to specific standards. Accountability requires transparency. As you pray to God there should be transparency about your thoughts and feelings.

Transparency with God brings change. You have to acknowledge and accept what God already knows. Acceptance is agreement and submission to the will of God, which will bring change to your life. You will also need God sent people in your life who will keep you accountable. Through prayer you will find and meet the right people for you to connect with in your season of singleness. As the verse says be sure to *"Trust in the Lord with all your heart. Lean not on your own understanding acknowledge Him in all your ways and He will direct your paths."*

JOURNAL SECTION

How is your prayer life?

Perfecting YOU!

Prayer and Accountability

Perfecting YOU!

Chapter Twelve

Current trends *in dating*

According to current research over the past several years the number of people getting married or being in relationships has been in decline. Today, more people are choosing to stay single. The FiveThirtyEight reports, "But how do Americans feel about the rise of single life? The new survey — and other research conducted within the past few years — shows that a decent chunk of people without a romantic partner are single by choice.

Perfecting YOU!

According to the Survey Center on American Life, single people were about as likely to say that they're not currently dating anyone and not looking to date (41 percent) as they were to say they were not dating someone but open to it (42 percent). 53 percent of Generation Z (Ages 12-27) also known as "Zoomers," 59 percent of Millennials (Ages 28-43), 64 percent of Generation X (Ages 44-59), and 73 percent of Baby Boomers (Ages 57-75) say they enjoy being single more than being in a relationship." From the statistics we can gather that relationships are being viewed differently. Relationships and marriages are not sought after like they once were. I believe the value of relationships and marriage has been tarnished by traumatizing experiences that have left long-lasting hurt and pain. Neglected hurt and pain has prevented many from committing to someone in a relationship or marriage, due to fear of being hurt and in more pain. The way to repair that, is to repair the single person. It starts with your relationship with yourself. Are you a healed and whole person? If not, you bring brokenness into relationships, which causes more broken people and broken relationships. We can also gather from the statistics that you can choose to be single and enjoy it.

For example According to Tinder Newsroom, "Millennials value freedom and independence. That's why 72% make a conscious decision to be single for a period of time." With many waiting longer to be married there is no specific age that you need to be married by. Singleness should be enjoyed and

Current Trends in Dating

in the midst of enjoying your singleness you can build strong friendships and relationships. Eventually, if you're looking, finding that one to marry will happen.

JOURNAL SECTION
Current trends

Current Trends in Dating

Perfecting YOU!

Current Trends in Dating

Perfecting YOU!

Chapter Thirteen

Encouraging messages *for singles*

"If you're single, use this time now to make the biggest impact you can for God's Kingdom. Enjoy how God uses you as a single adult to show His love to others because you are in a unique place to minister to others where married adults could not!"

- Jack Graham

"I'm not saying that every single needs to pack up and move overseas. I think that'd be great, but doesn't necessarily have to happen. But how is your life here in this moment going to trust in the sovereignty of God, His plans, His grace, His mercy in your life, and ask God, 'How can my singleness, right now, as long as I've got the gift of singleness, God, how can it count for Your glory?' And this is a question worth asking. It's a question that the Gospel gives us the privilege of asking."

- David Platt

Perfecting YOU!

"Some will remain wonderfully content as a single adult all their lives, while others pray, ache, and long for a marriage partner. My exhortation is strong: Don't allow that desire to hurry you into making a commitment you could live to regret. Take the time prayerfully and wisely to choose a mate. I wish I could invite all the impatient singles to come sit in on a heated marriage counseling session. You would quickly change your tune! There are a lot of people who are married to partners they would love for YOU to have. Matter of fact, their partners would say they are readily available! And believe me, you don't want them either. There's something a lot worse than not having a marriage partner, and that's having the wrong one. So, please, be patient."

- Chuck Swindoll

"Singleness is not a disease in need of a cure. God can lead you into a time (or lifetime) of fruitful ministry as a single person. And if you at times feel frustration over an earnest longing to be married, remember this time of being single is part of God's good plan too. The church, for her part, needs to do a better job reaching out to singles, not treating them like misfits or as simply married people waiting to happen."

- Kevin DeYoung

"Some of the greatest people who ever served God were single. Rejoice in all the gifts God has given you, including your singleness. Seeking marriage is not wrong, but don't let that search dominate your life. We must not make finding a marriage partner the supreme goal of our lives by putting all our energies into searching for a mate. Learn contentment, for it is great gain."

- David Jeremiah, from his book *"Sanctuary: Finding Moments of*

Refuge in the Presence of God"

"...*the experience of singleness should not be reduced to a time of preparation for marriage. It should rather be seen as a platform of great opportunity for the advancement of the kingdom of God. If singleness is a stage of life, it ought to be viewed as preparatory for whatever comes next in the sovereign will of God – whether marriage or continued singleness. And far from waiting for marriage to get on with life, single Christians should maximize the potential of their state for growing in their devotion to God and serving Him for so long as they are single.* "

- J. Robin Maxson, *retired senior pastor, from his book "I Do or Do I?"*

"*For a long time I thought of Psalm 37:4 as the single person's verse of hope. How many times have we heard this verse quoted to or by a single person and interpreted as, 'If I just get close to God, then He'll give me what I really want – a husband!' We might think that if we give God our obedience and interest and compliments, we can get what we want from Him in return. But delighting in God is not a way to get what we want from Him. This is manipulation and bribery. Genuine delight has no ulterior motive, no additional demands. If we see this verse as a formula for getting what we want from God, we're settling for much less than what God is offering. God wants to change what we want. He wants to free us from the slavery of wanting what will never completely satisfy us. He wants to give us what He knows will completely satisfy us forever: Himself.*"

- Nancy Guthrie

Perfecting YOU!

"Christianity's founder, Jesus Christ, and leading theologian, St. Paul, were both single their entire lives. Single adults cannot be seen as somehow less fully formed or realized human beings than married persons because Jesus Christ, a single man, was the perfect man (Hebrews 4:15; 1 Peter 2:22)."

- Tim Keller

"...the Bible gives us a very compelling vision for the joy of singleness and devotion to God that seems to me to be neglected by and large…we're all single before we're married, and how we live as singles has great impact on how we subsequently live as married folks."

- Thabiti Anyabwile

"To know God, to know beyond the shadow of a doubt that He is sovereign and that my life is in His care: this is the unshakable foundation on which I stay my soul. Such knowledge has deep significance for the single Christian."

- Margaret Clarkson

JOURNAL SECTION

Perfecting YOU!

Encouraging Messages for Singles

Perfecting YOU!

Chapter Fourteen

Dating and Marriage *Goals*

What are your dating and marriage goals? Write some goals you have for dating and marriage and keep track of your progress. Below are some of my dating and marriage goals.

My Dating Goals

1. My ultimate dating goal and purpose for dating is to be married. In this season of my life I am dating to marry.
2. I seek to let God promote my relationship status. I want to make Godly connections and friendships through dating. From the position of friendship, I will then allow God to promote the relationship to anything beyond that.
3. I seek to grow as a person through the dating process and confirm that I am truly ready for marriage. Dating can be challenging and will reveal things about yourself, good and bad. Dating will also reveal if you are truly ready for

marriage.
4. I seek to clearly communicate who I am. While dating someone, I want to clearly communicate who I am, so they know what they might be getting themselves into lol. However, all jokes aside, it's important that anyone I'm dating have an understanding of who I am and where I'm going in life, in order for them to properly assess if they are headed in the same direction.
5. Lastly, I want to have fun, meet new people, and enjoy the process!

Goals in Preparation for Marriage

1. I seek to be truly single. In preparation for marriage, I want to make sure I am truly single. My goal is to assess my life and disconnect from anything that could possibly be a hindrance in my marriage.
2. I seek to continue to learn about marriage. In preparation for marriage, I have been learning about it through various teachings and will continue to grow in my knowledge and understanding of it.
3. I seek to enhance and grow in my communication skills. Good Communication is important in life and will be important in a marriage. In preparation for marriage, I have been confronting how I communicate. Through confrontation I have been able to identify places of communication that can be strengthened.

Goals for Marriage

1. I seek to be an effective leader. In a marriage, I desire to be an effective leader of my wife and family. I believe good leadership starts with self. Can you effectively lead yourself? If you can effectively lead yourself, you can do the same with others. Leadership also starts with submission and obedience to God's leadership and those He has placed as leaders in your life. I will continue to assess my leadership and where I need to grow and make adjustments. I will also continue to assess my submission and obedience to God and leaders, in order to continue to grow in my leadership.

2. I seek to have a vision for my marriage. In a marriage, I believe there should be a vision of what that marriage should be and where it is going. Vision brings purpose. Without a purpose, I imagine it would just be two people hanging out with each other for the rest of their lives. Before entering marriage with someone I want to establish a vision and allow that vision to grow in the marriage. Vision will reveal purpose and keep us moving forward.

3. Lastly, I seek to have a marriage that is built on Faith in God. I want to build it on a firm foundation. Two people coming together in marriage is a huge leap of faith. If two people trust in their foundation (God), then I believe whatever that marriage goes through they can be confident it will stand. Yes, it will bend at times, but it won't break because the foundation is sure.

Perfecting YOU!

JOURNAL SECTION

What are your dating and marriage goals?

Dating and Marriage Goals

Perfecting YOU!

Dating and Marriage Goals

SCRIPTURES

Hope in Loneliness

It can often feel heavy to carry the weight of loneliness, but God always offers a glimmer of hope. His Word is full of promises that remind us that our loneliness is temporary and that He has plans to prosper us. Having this hope in our hearts allows us to rise above the pain of solitude, even when it tries to overwhelm us. God's declarations bring us assurance and continue to fuel our faith in His faithfulness.

For I know the plans I have for you," declares the LORD, "plans to prosper you and not to harm you, plans to give you hope and a future. Jeremiah 29:11

The LORD is close to the brokenhearted and saves those who are crushed in spirit. – Psalm 34:18

God's Presence in Loneliness

When we feel lonely, it's often during those times we need to remember that God is always with us. We are never truly by ourselves because His presence surrounds us, comforting us in moments of solitude. The Bible shows us that God walks alongside us, even in our darkest days. We can find solace in His promises, for He assures us that we are His beloved children.

Let us lean on this powerful truth and feel His loving embrace during our lonely moments.

Comforting One Another

During times of loneliness, it's important for us to remind one another about the love of Christ. We are called to support those who feel alone in our communities, families, and friendships. As we reach out with kindness an Dd compassion, we can truly be the hands and feet of Jesus. Together, we can build a network of love that uplifts the weary heart and lets the lonely know they are not forgotten.

Who comforts us in all our troubles, so that we can comfort those in any trouble. 2 Corinthians 1:4

Jesus Understands Our Loneliness

One of the most comforting truths is that Jesus understands loneliness. In His time on earth, He faced abandonment and solitude, which brings us assurance that He knows our struggles. His experience in suffering gives us an advocate who reaches out to us in prayer and lifts us in our times of need. When we feel alone, we can bring our burdens to Him, knowing He is fully aware of our pain.

But a time is coming and in fact has come when you will be

scattered, each to your own home. You will leave me all alone. Yet I am not alone, for my Father is with me. – John 16:32

Finding Joy in Solitude

While loneliness can often lead to sorrow, we can choose to embrace solitude as a time for personal growth and connection with God. Rather than seeing this time as solely negative, we can transform moments of isolation into opportunities for spiritual development. By dedicating ourselves to prayer, reflection, and Bible study during these solitary times, we open ourselves to receiving joy and wisdom from God.

I rise before dawn and cry for help; I have put my hope in your word. Psalm 119:147

Submit to God and be at peace with him; in this way, prosperity will come to you. Job 22:21

God's Faithfulness to the Lonely

Through true trials of loneliness, we can lean on the unchanging faithfulness of God. His promise to uphold us does not waver, and we can take comfort in His presence. We are assured that God not only acknowledges our loneliness but actively comforts and carries us through it. Let us hold on to His faithfulness, believing that He is forever with us even when the world feels vacant.

Bible verses about strength

John 16:33: I have said these things to you, that in me you may have peace. In the world you will have tribulation. But take heart; I have overcome the world.

Isaiah 41:10: So do not fear, for I am with you; do not be dismayed, for I am your God. I will strengthen you and help you; I will uphold you with my righteous right hand.

Philippians 4:6-7: Do not be anxious about anything, but in every situation, by prayer and petition, with thanksgiving, present your requests to God. And the peace of God, which transcends all understanding, will guard your hearts and your minds in Christ Jesus.

Psalm 34:6-8: This poor man called, and the LORD heard him; he saved him out of all his troubles. The angel of the LORD encamps around those who fear him, and he delivers them. Taste and see that the LORD is good; blessed is the one who takes refuge in him.

Romans 8:28: And we know that in all things God works for the good of those who love him, who have been called according to his purpose.

Joshua 1:9: Have I not commanded you? Be strong and courageous. Do not be frightened, and do not be dismayed, for the Lord your God is with you wherever you go.

Matthew 6:31-34: So do not worry, saying, 'What shall we eat?' or 'What shall we drink?' or 'What shall we wear?' For the pagans run after all these things, and your heavenly Father knows that you need them. But seek first his kingdom and his righteousness, and all these things will be given to you as well. Therefore do not worry about tomorrow, for tomorrow will worry about itself. Each day has enough trouble of its own.

2 Timothy 1:7: For God gave us a spirit not of fear but of power and love and self-control.

Philippians 4:13: I can do all things through him who strengthens me.

Psalm 37:4: Delight yourself in the Lord, and he will give you the desires of your heart.

Psalm 28:7: The Lord is my strength and my shield; in him my heart trusts, and I am helped; my heart exults, and with my song

I give thanks to him.

Mark 11:24: Therefore I tell you, whatever you ask in prayer, believe that you have received it, and it will be yours.

Psalm 34:4: I sought the Lord, and he answered me and delivered me from all my fears.

Romans 15:13: May the God of hope fill you with all joy and peace in believing, so that by the power of the Holy Spirit you may abound in hope.

1 Thessalonians 5:11: Therefore encourage one another and build one another up, just as you are doing.

1 Corinthians 15:58: Therefore, my beloved brothers, be steadfast, immovable, always abounding in the work of the Lord, knowing that in the Lord your labor is not in vain.

Romans 15:4: For whatever was written in former days was written for our instruction, that through endurance and through the encouragement of the Scriptures we might have hope.

Matthew 11:28: Come to me, all who labor and are heavy laden, and I will give you rest.

Isaiah 43:2: When you pass through the waters, I will be with you; and through the rivers, they shall not overwhelm you; when you walk through fire you shall not be burned, and the flame shall not consume you.

Psalm 23:4: Even though I walk through the valley of the shadow of death, I will fear no evil, for you are with me; your rod and your staff, they comfort me.

Bible Verses About Hope

God promises can encourage us when we lose hope. These Scriptures will remind you of the hope that we have in Jesus Christ - a hope for eternity but also a hope for today to be blessed and favored!

"May the God of hope fill you with all joy and peace as you trust in him, so that you may overflow with hope by the power of the Holy Spirit." Romans 15:13

"And the God of all grace, who called you to his eternal glory in Christ, after you have suffered a little while, will himself restore you and make you strong, firm and steadfast." 1 Peter 5:10

"Let us hold unswervingly to the hope we profess, for he who promised is faithful." Hebrews 10:23

"I pray that the eyes of your heart may be enlightened in order that you may know the hope to which he has called you, the riches of his glorious inheritance in his holy people," Ephesians 1:13

"We remember before our God and Father your work produced by faith, your labor prompted by love, and your endurance inspired by hope in our Lord Jesus Christ." 1 Thessalonians 1:3

"being confident of this, that he who began a good work in you will carry it on to completion until the day of Christ Jesus." Philippians 1:6

"I wait for the LORD, my whole being waits, and in his word I put my hope." Psalm 130:5

"And hope does not put us to shame, because God's love has been poured out into our hearts through the Holy Spirit, who has been given to us." Romans 5:5

Top Bible Verses for Faith during Hardships

Isaiah 41:10
Fear not, for I am with you; be not dismayed, for I am your God; I will strengthen you, I will help you, I will uphold you with my righteous right hand.

Proverbs 3:5-6

Trust in the Lord with all your heart, and do not lean on your own understanding. In all your ways acknowledge him, and he will make straight your paths.

Hebrews 11:6

And without faith it is impossible to please him, for whoever would draw near to God must believe that he exists and that he rewards those who seek him.

Hebrews 11:1

Now faith is the assurance of things hoped for, the conviction of things not seen.

Psalm 46:10

"Be still, and know that I am God. I will be exalted among the nations, I will be exalted in the earth!"

JOURNAL SECTION

References

Singleness is the First Step
Munroe, Myles. "99% of Singles will fail in marriage because of this." Youtube, Relationship Connect, Thursday August 21, 2024. https://www.youtube.com/watch?v=CLUe4FTU9ck

Alone vs. Lonely
"Singles, do this while waiting on your spouse." Youtube, Vlad, Savchuk, Saturday June 14, 2024, https://www.youtube.com/watch?v=ukdOJEXQRIU&t=765s.

Merriam-Webster, 1996, https://www.merriam-webster.com.

Holy Bible, King James Version Large Print Compact Edition, 2016, Print.

"Encouraging Quotes about Singleness-Part 1" Single, Unexpectedly, 29 Sept.2013, https://singleunexpectedly.blogspot.com/search/label/Encouraging%20Quotes%20about%20Singleness%20-%20Part%201

"Encouraging Quotes about Singleness-Part 2" Single, Unexpectedly, 11 Mar. 2014, https://singleunexpectedly.blogspot.com/search/label/Encouraging%20Quotes%20about%20Singleness%20-%20Part%202

"Encouraging Quotes about Singleness-Part 3" Single, Unexpectedly, 7 Jun. 2014 https://singleunexpectedly.blogspot.

com/search/label/Encouraging%20Quotes%20about%20 Singleness%20-%20Part%203

"Encouraging Quotes about Singleness-Part 5" Single, Unexpectedly, 8 Nov.2014, https://singleunexpectedly. blogspot.com/search/label/Encouraging%20Quotes%20 about%20Singleness%20-%20Part%205

"Encouraging Quotes about Singleness-Part 6" Single, Unexpectedly, 3 July.2015, https://singleunexpectedly.blogspot. com/search/label/Encouraging%20Quotes%20about%20 Singleness%20-%20Part%206

Chandel, Shivani "217 Best Quotes About Being Single" Style Craze 11, February 2025, https://www.stylecraze.com/articles/being-single-quotes/

www.ingramcontent.com/pod-product-compliance
Lightning Source LLC
Chambersburg PA
CBHW070148080526
44586CB00015B/1890